I0467615

# How To Draw Realistic Skulls Volume 3

## Simple Guide to Drawing Skulls

How to Draw Skulls

By : Gala Publication

2

Published By :

# Gala Publication
© Copyright 2015 – Gala Publication

ISBN-13: **978-1522785620**
ISBN-10: **1522785620**

# Table of Contents

# BANDIT SKULL

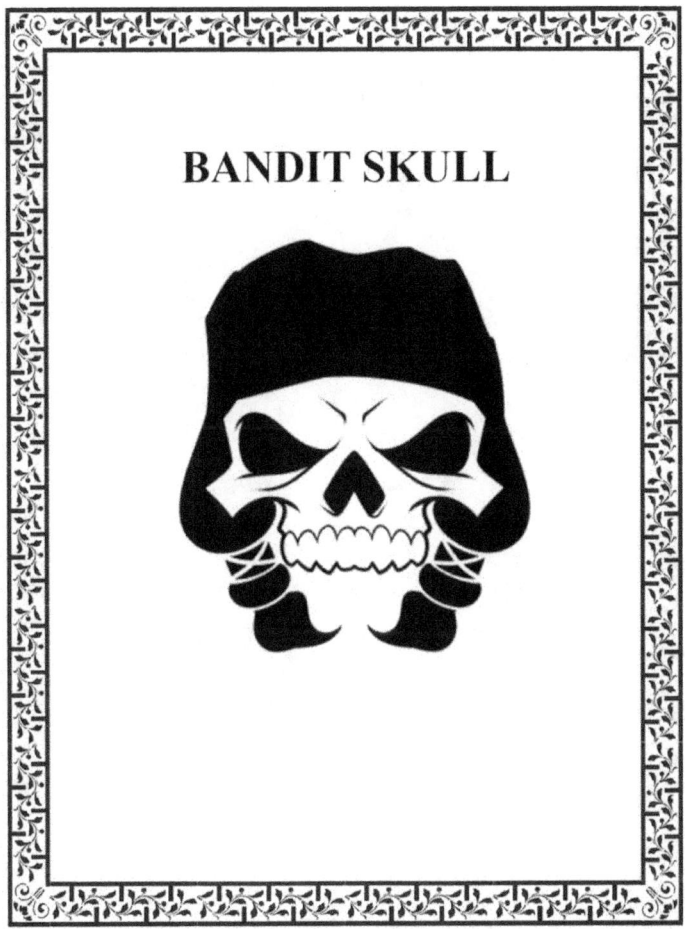

# STEP 1

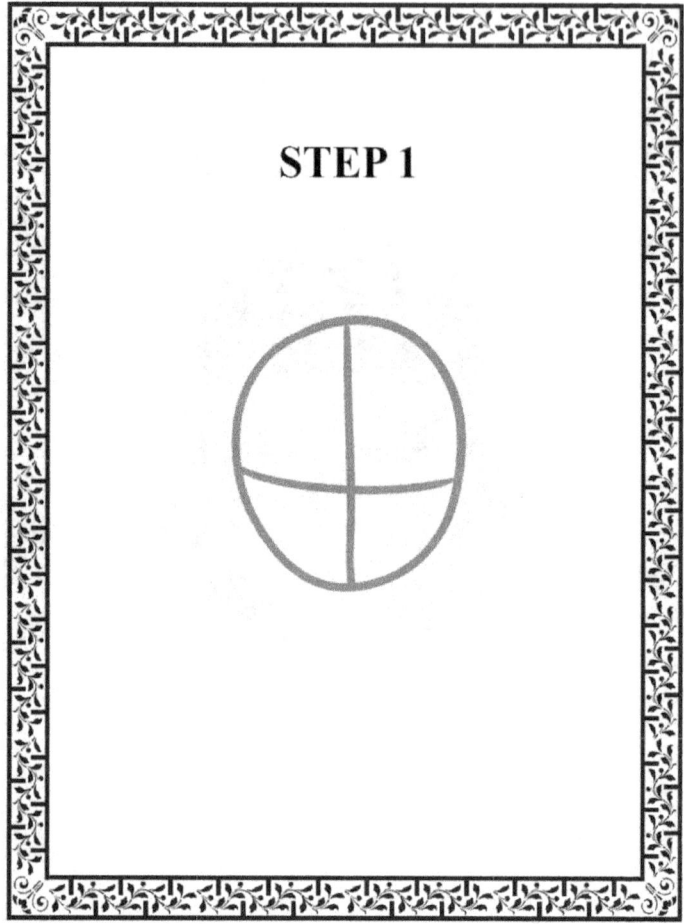

# STEP 2

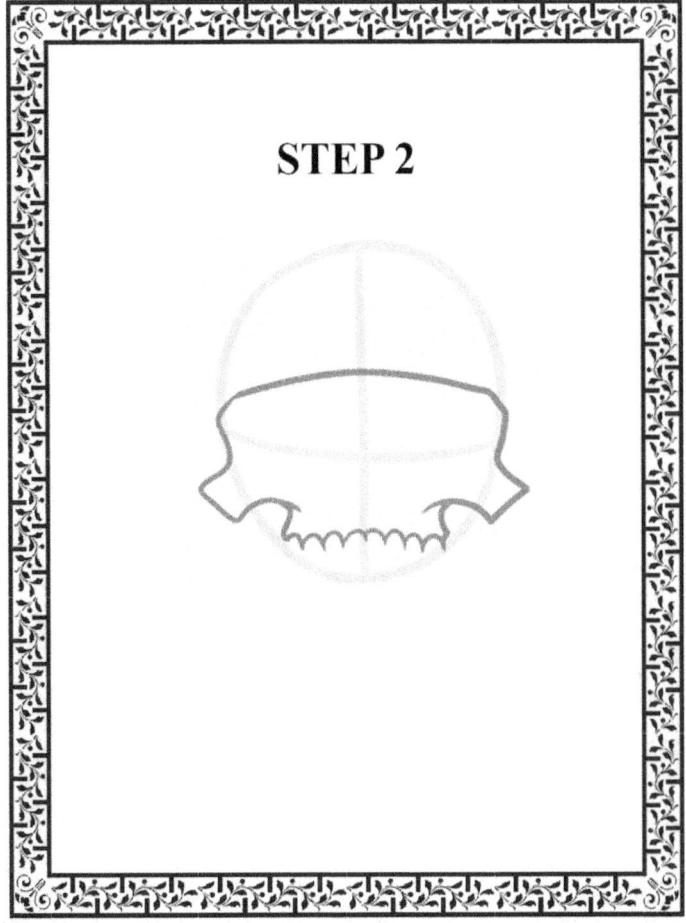

# STEP 3

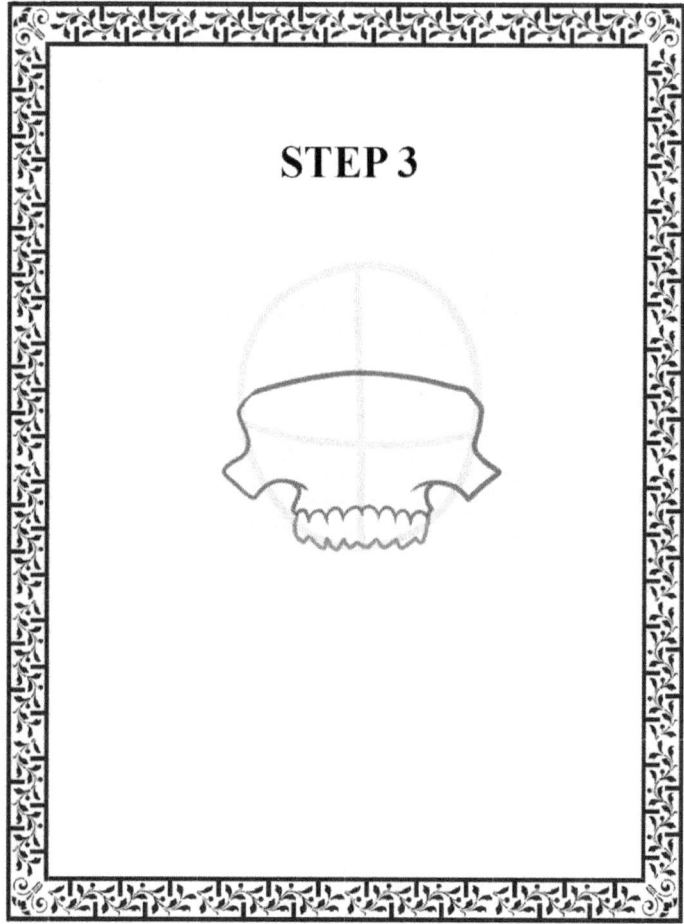

# STEP 4

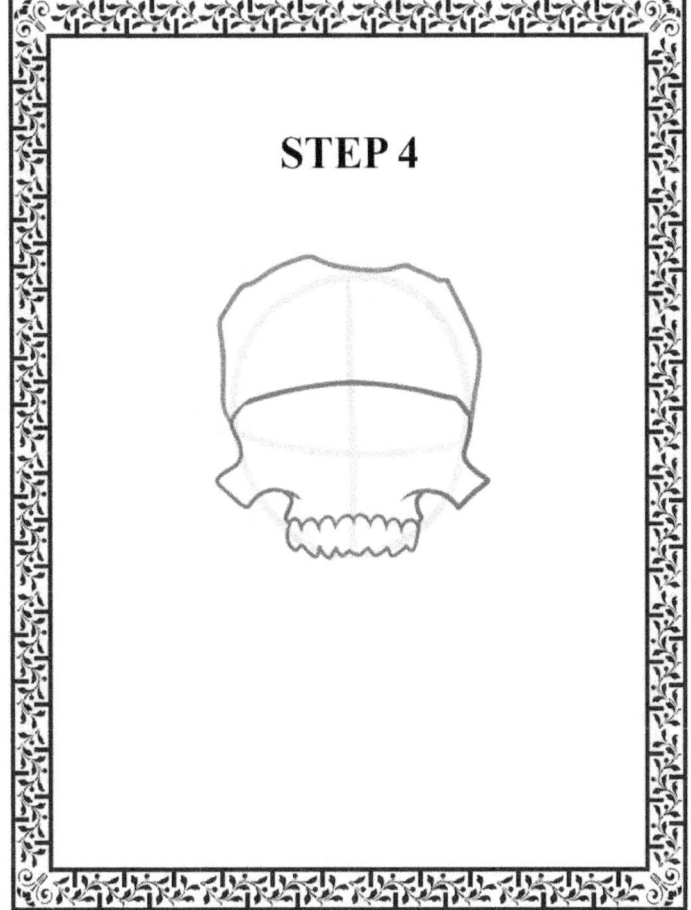

# STEP 5

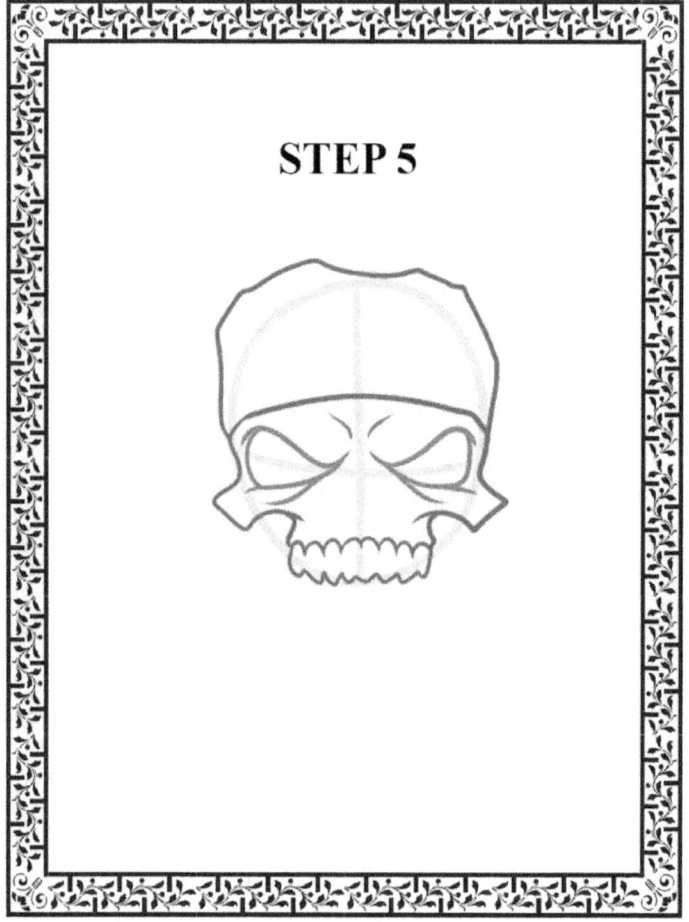

# STEP 6

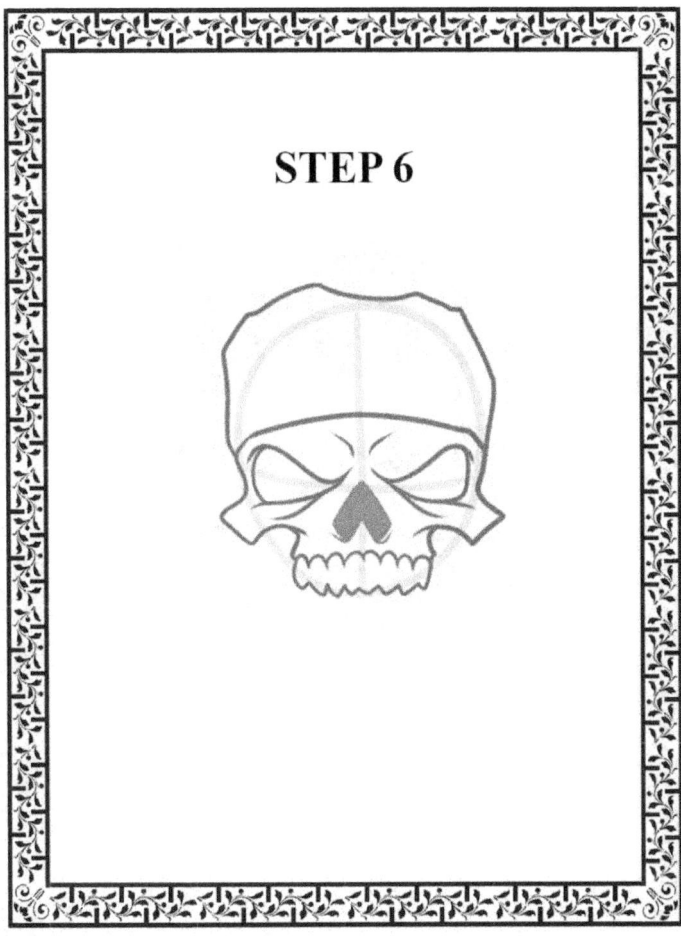

# STEP 7

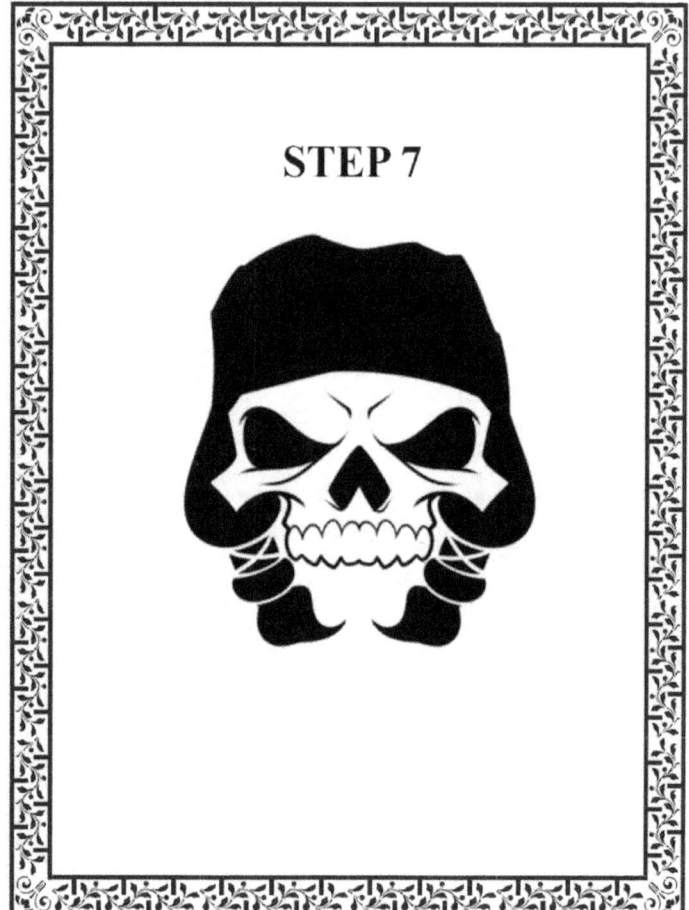

# CANDY SKULL

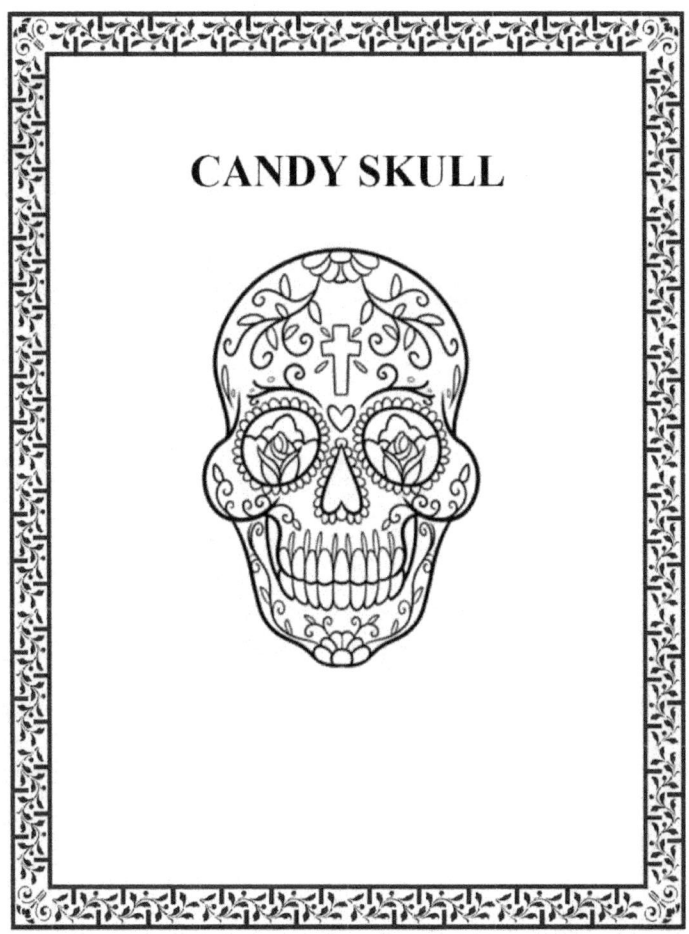

# STEP 1

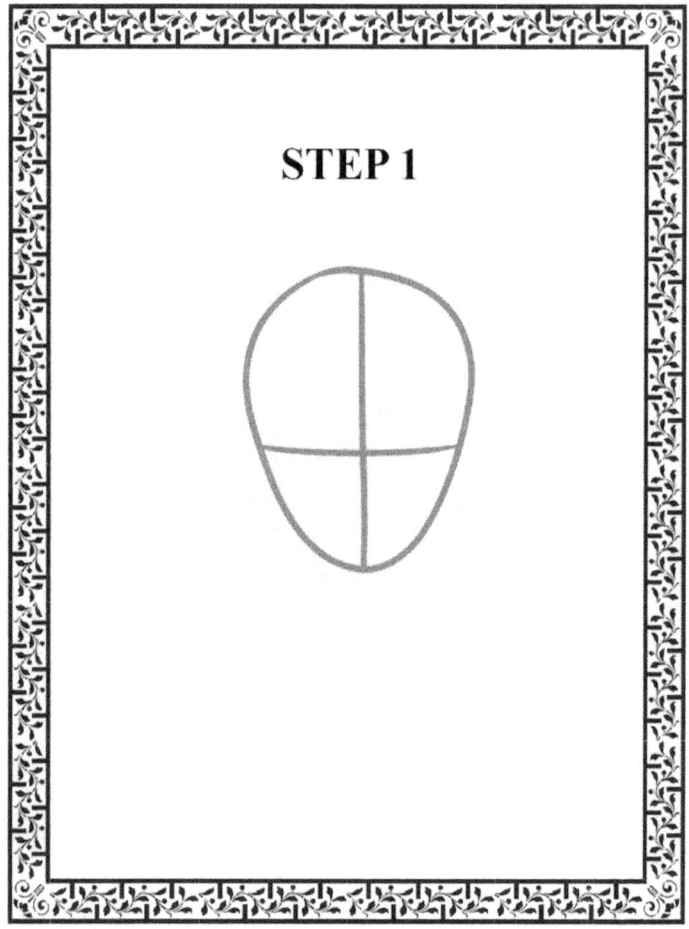

# STEP 2

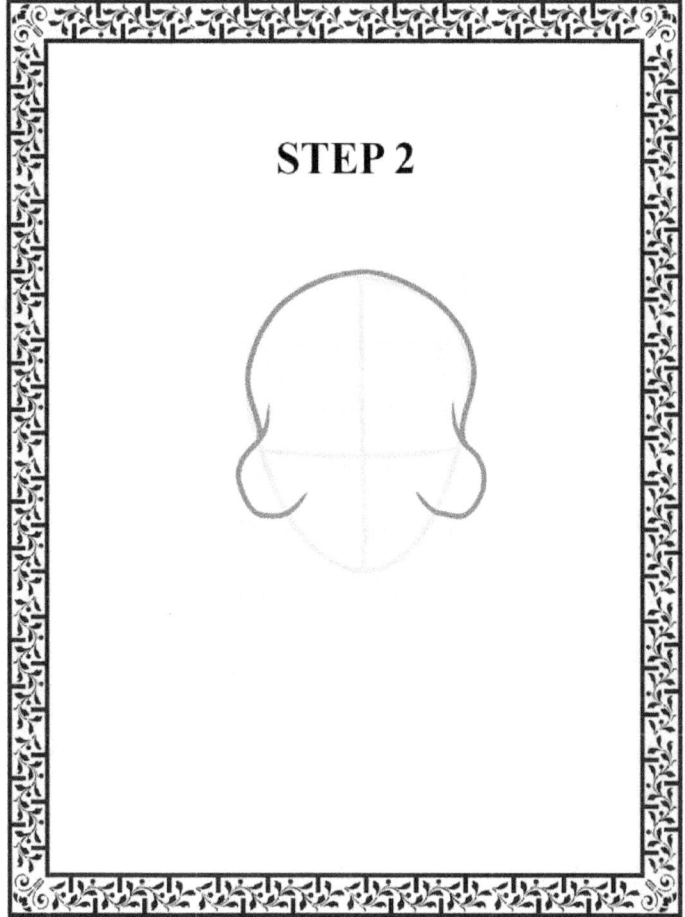

# STEP 3

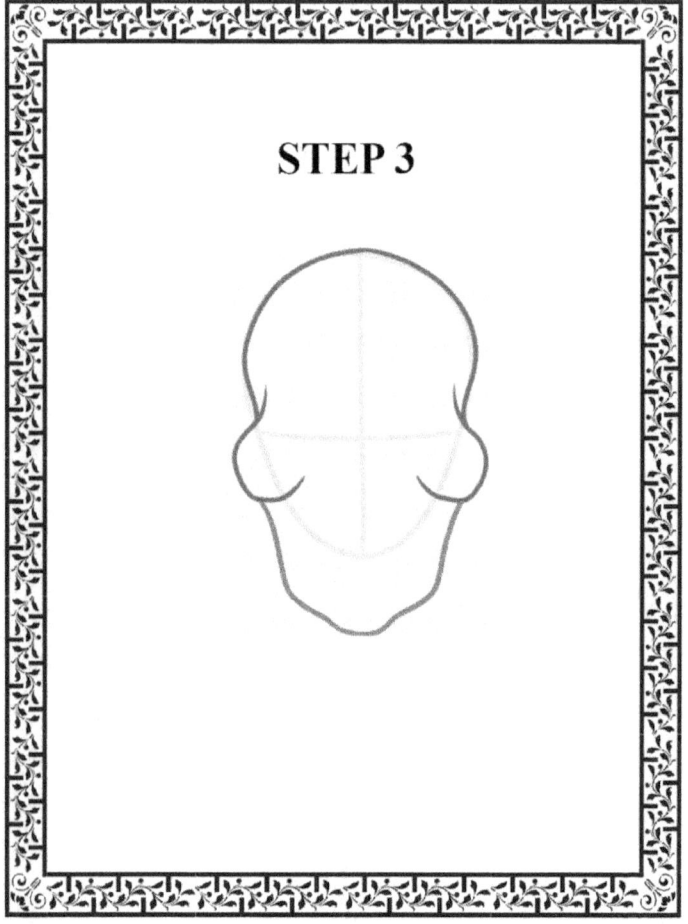

# STEP 4

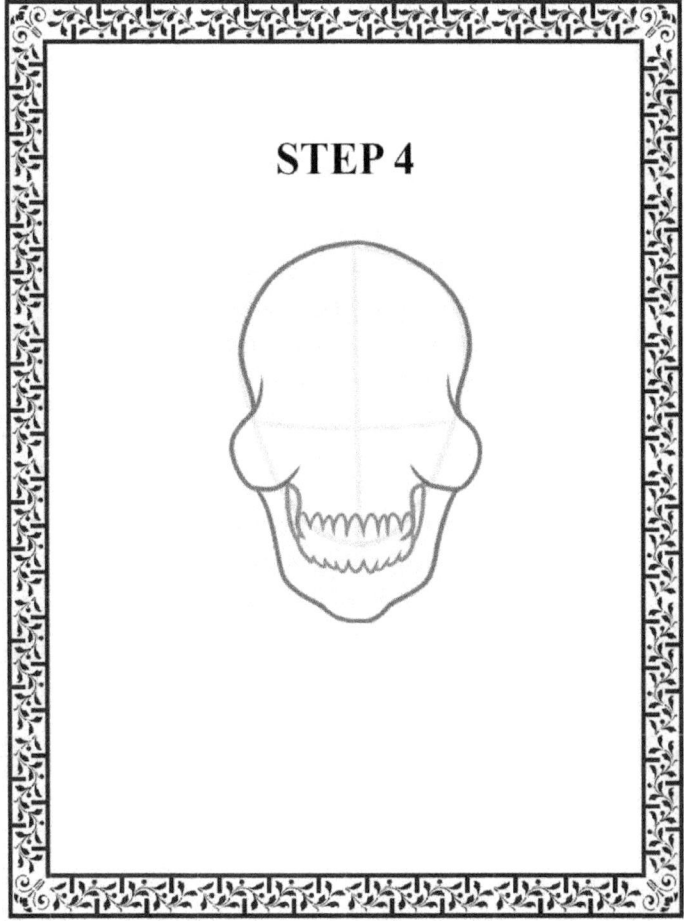

# STEP 5

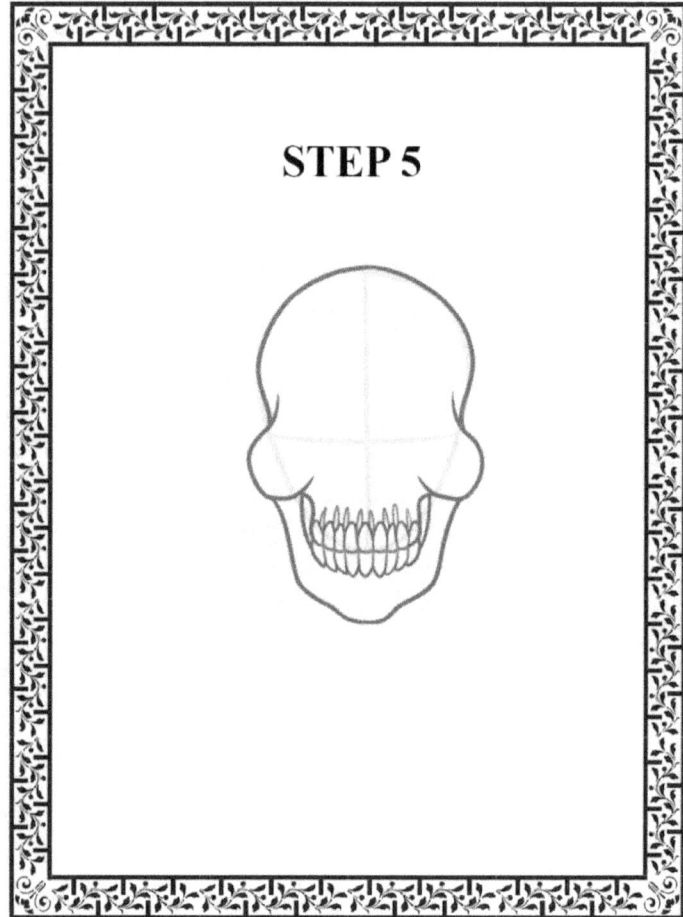

# STEP 6

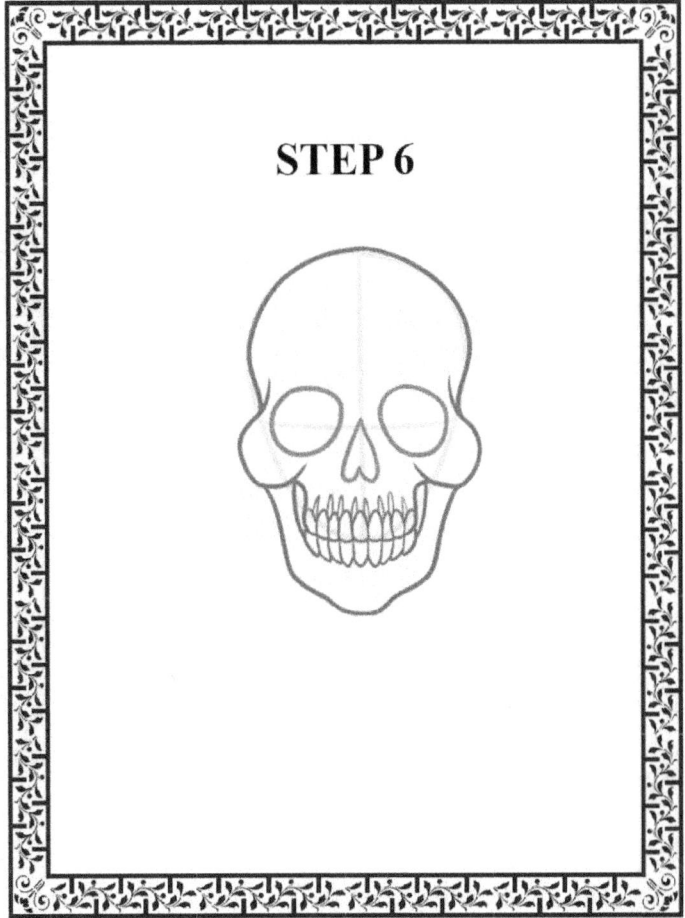

# STEP 7

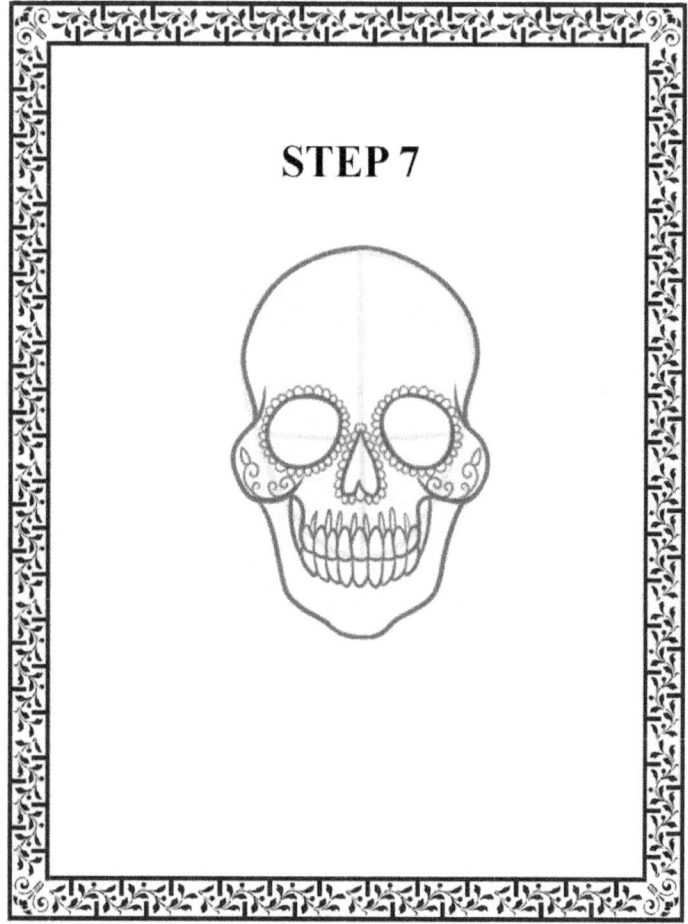

# STEP 8

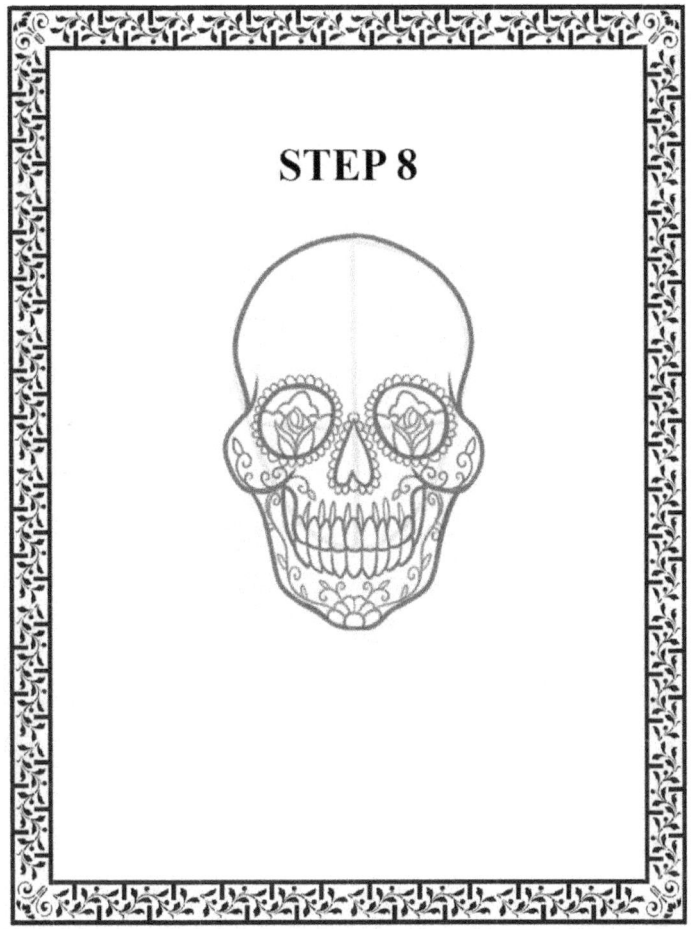

# STEP 9

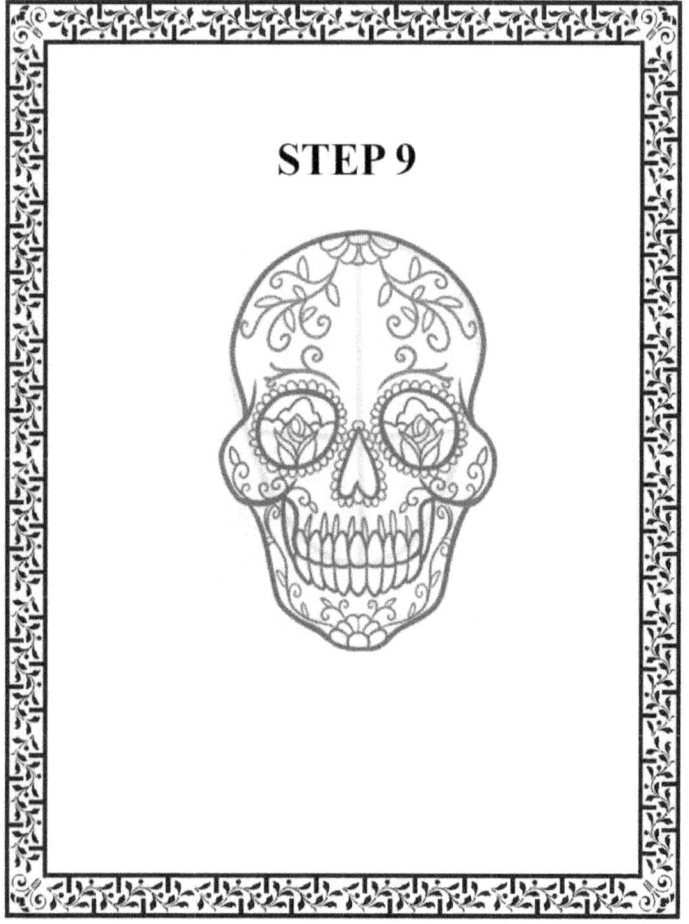

# STEP 10

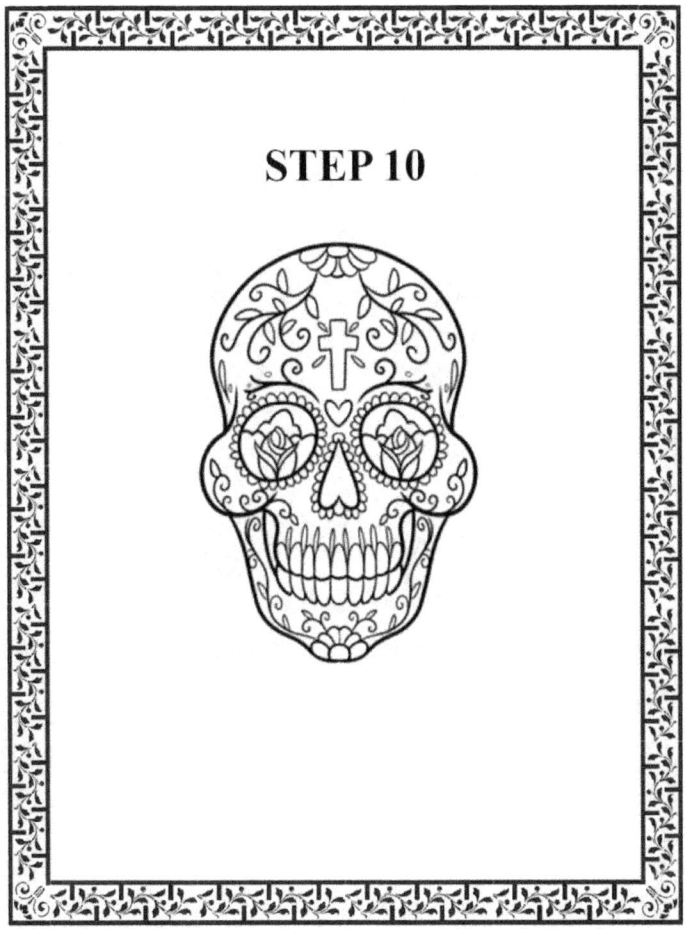

# HELLO KITTY
# SKULL

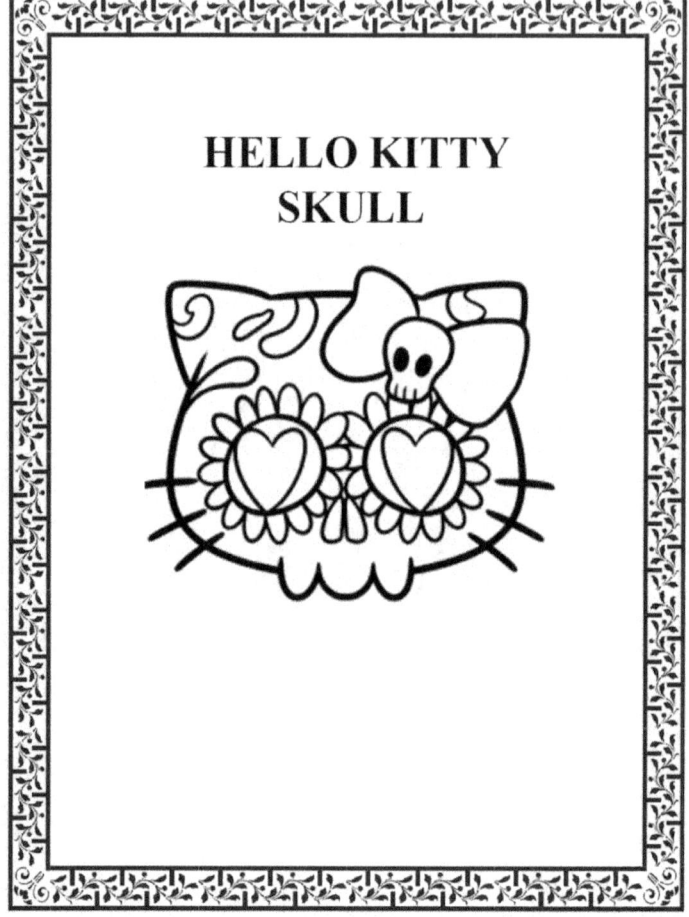

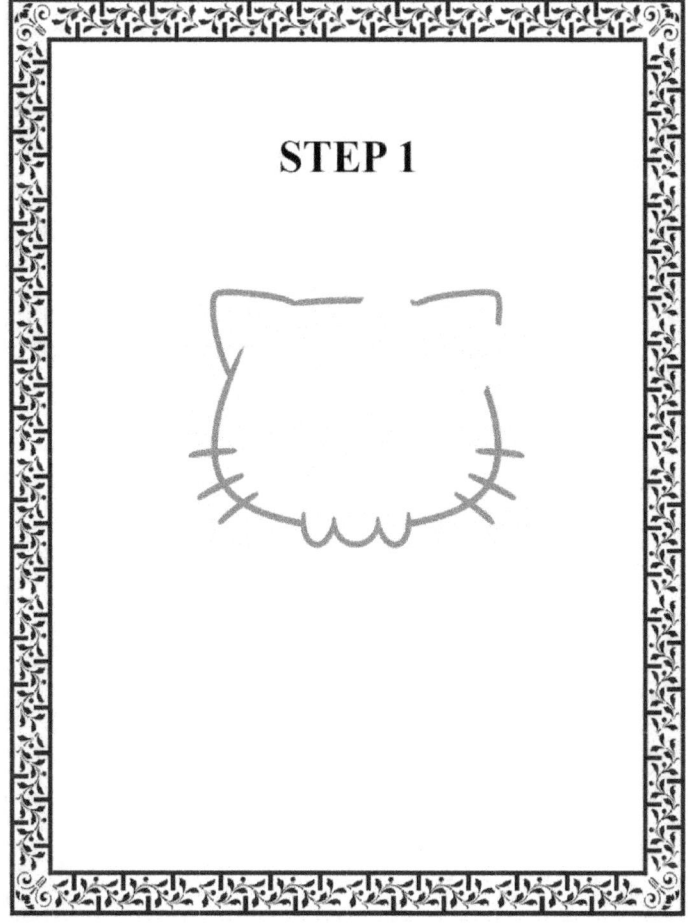

# STEP 1

# STEP 2

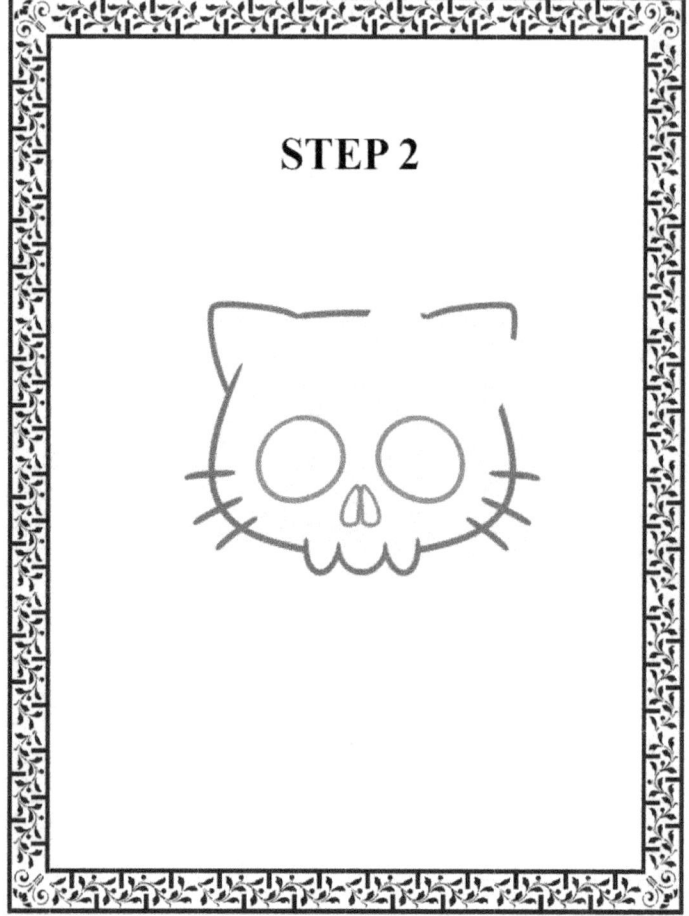

# STEP 3

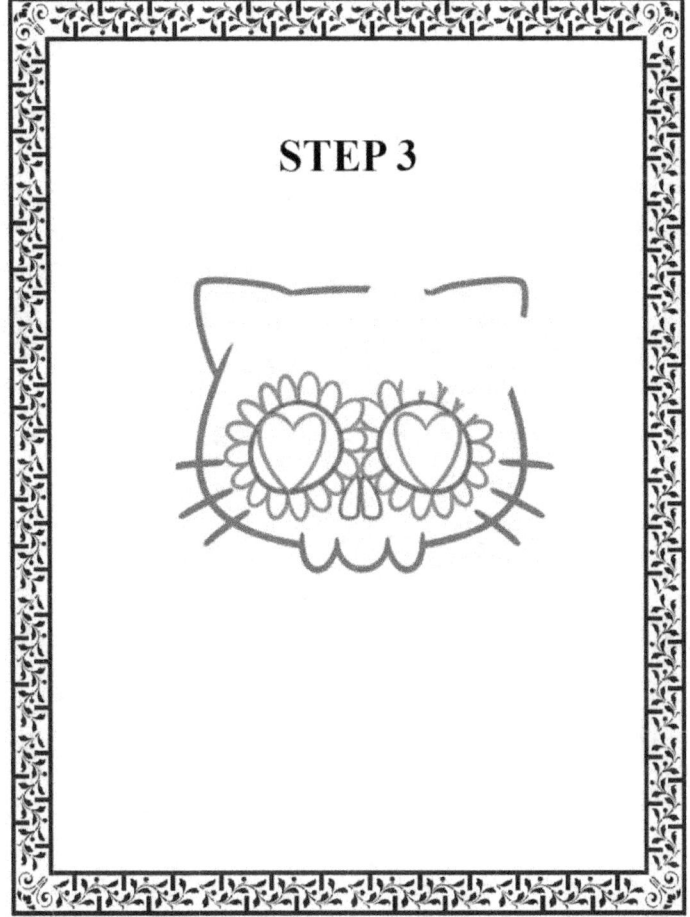

# STEP 4

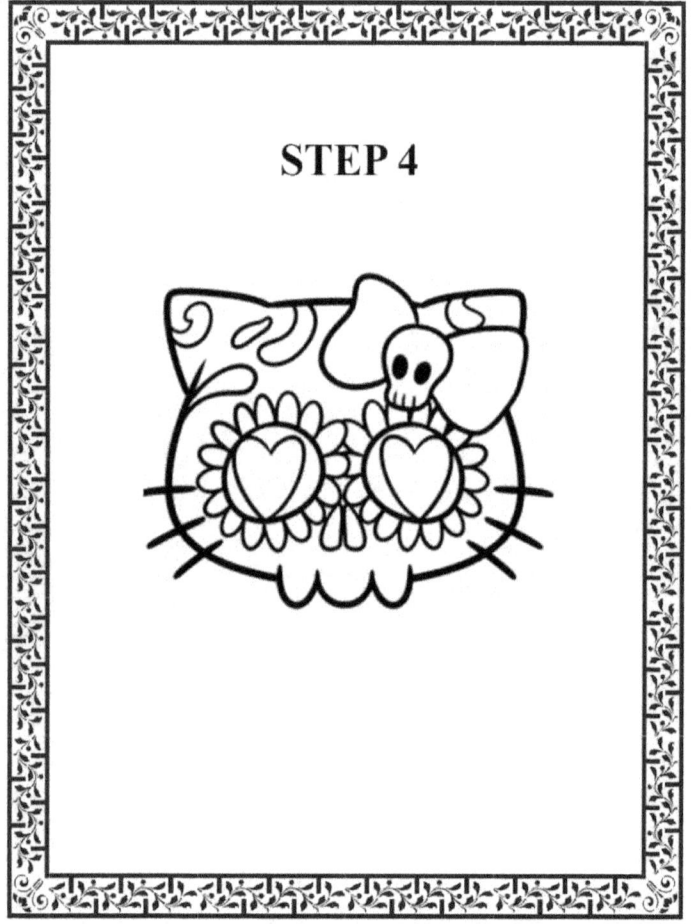

# ONE EYE SKULL

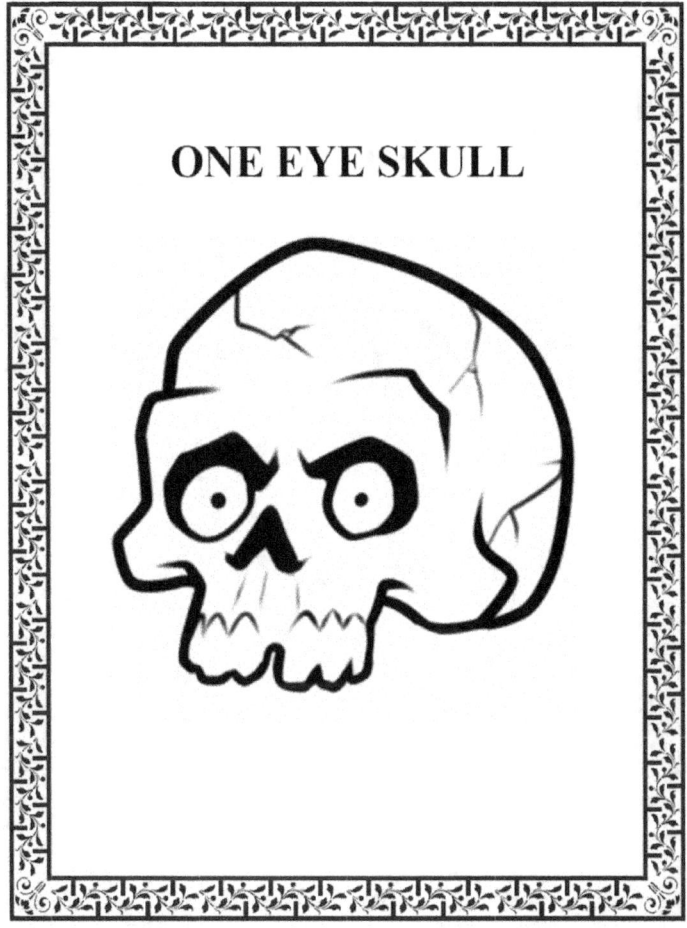

# STEP 1

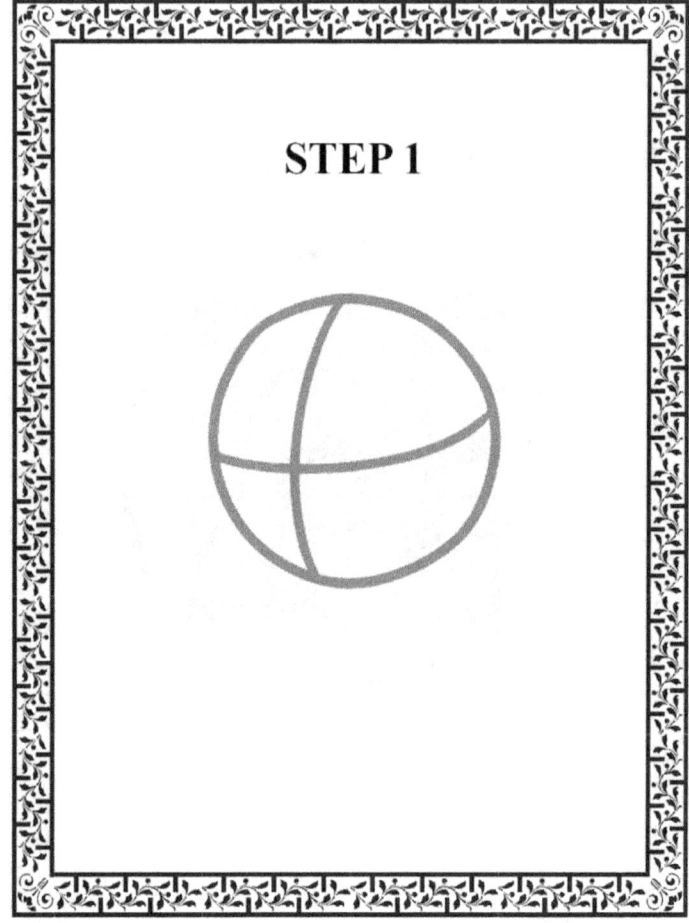

# STEP 2

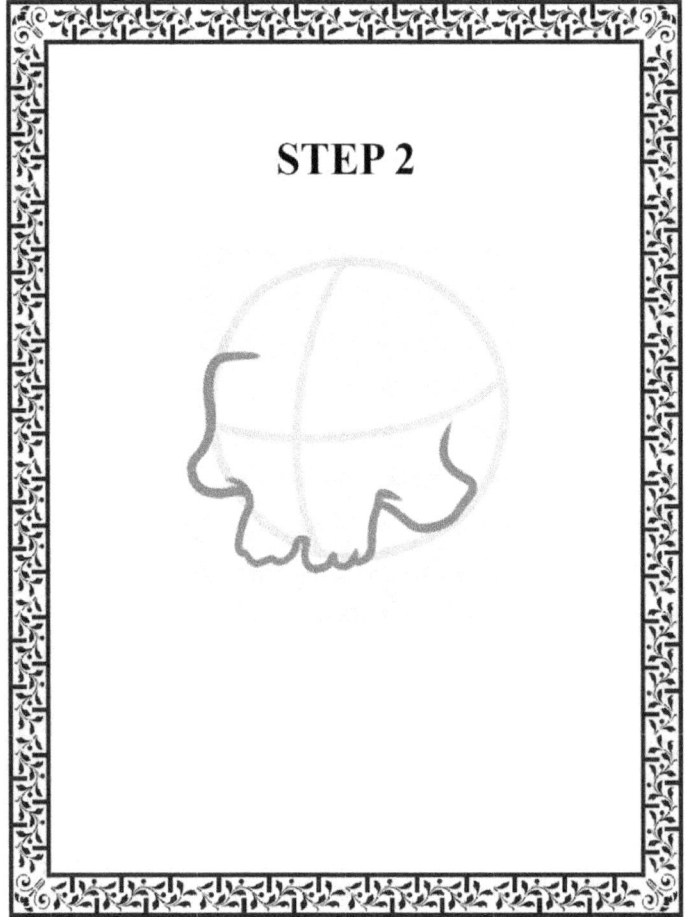

# STEP 3

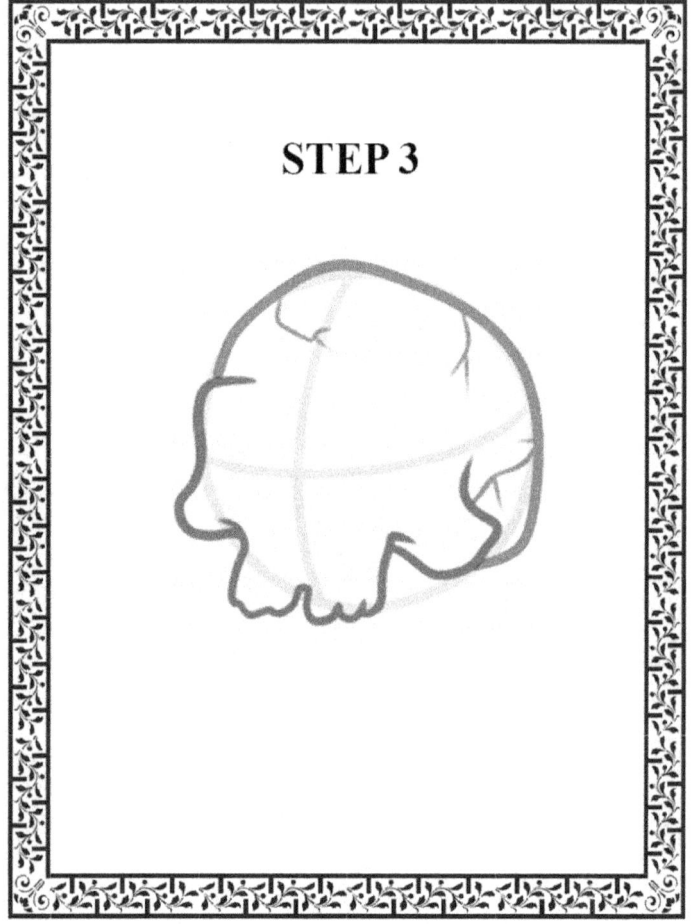

# STEP 4

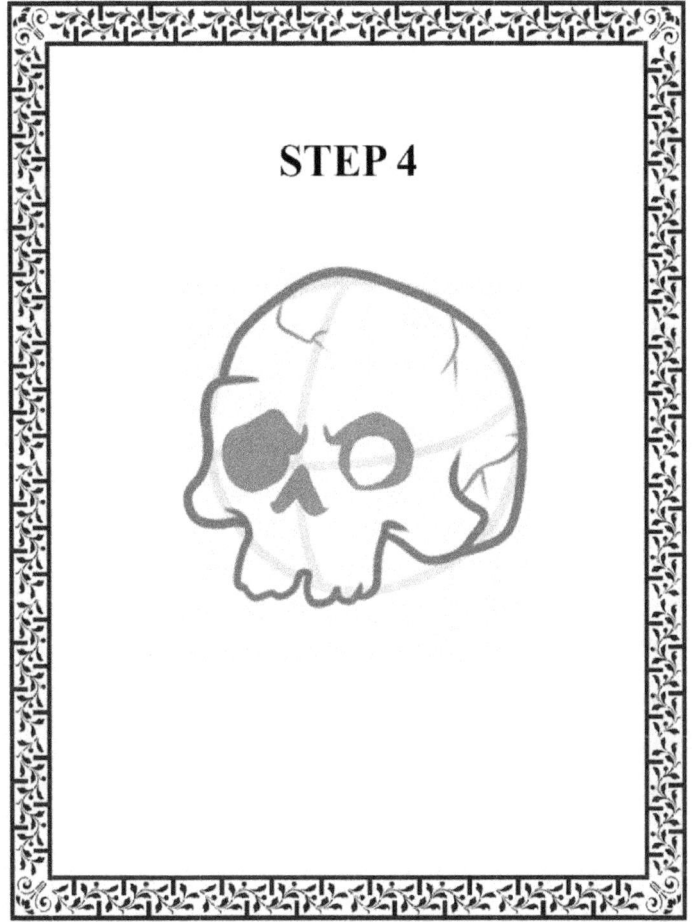

# STEP 5

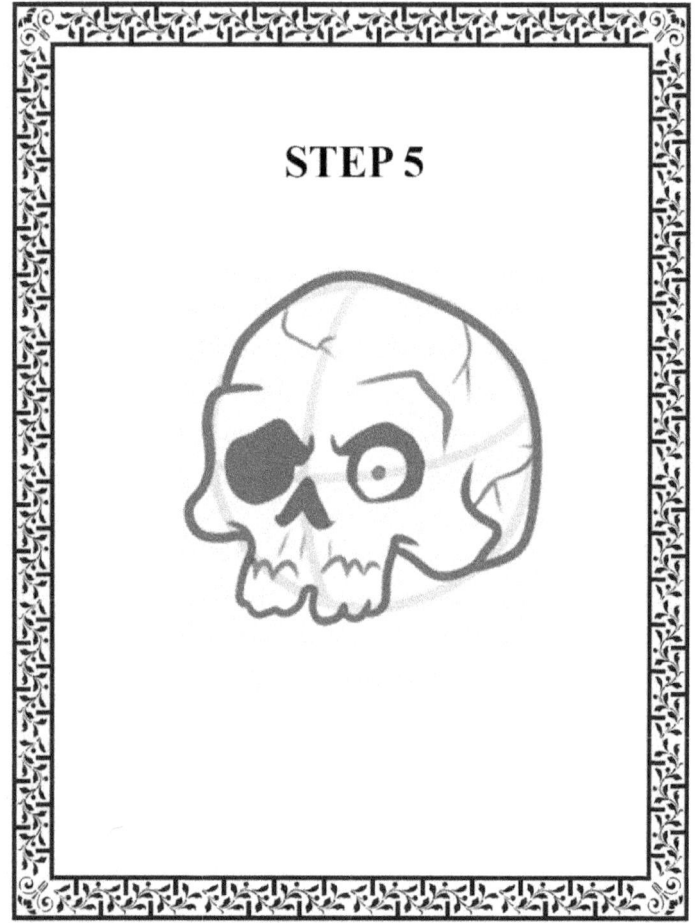

# STEP 6

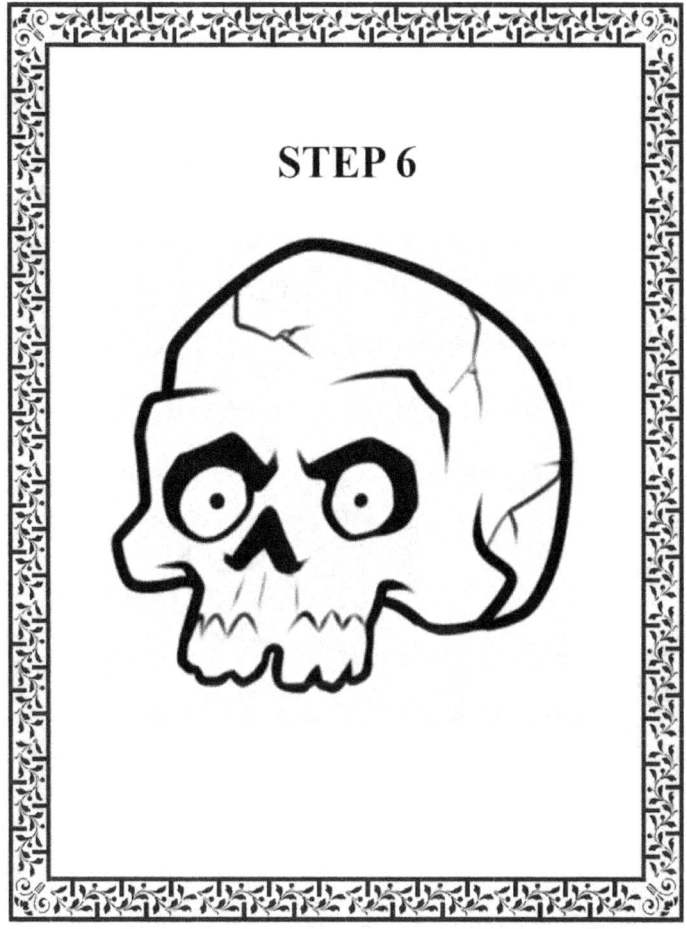

# PINKIE PIE SKULL

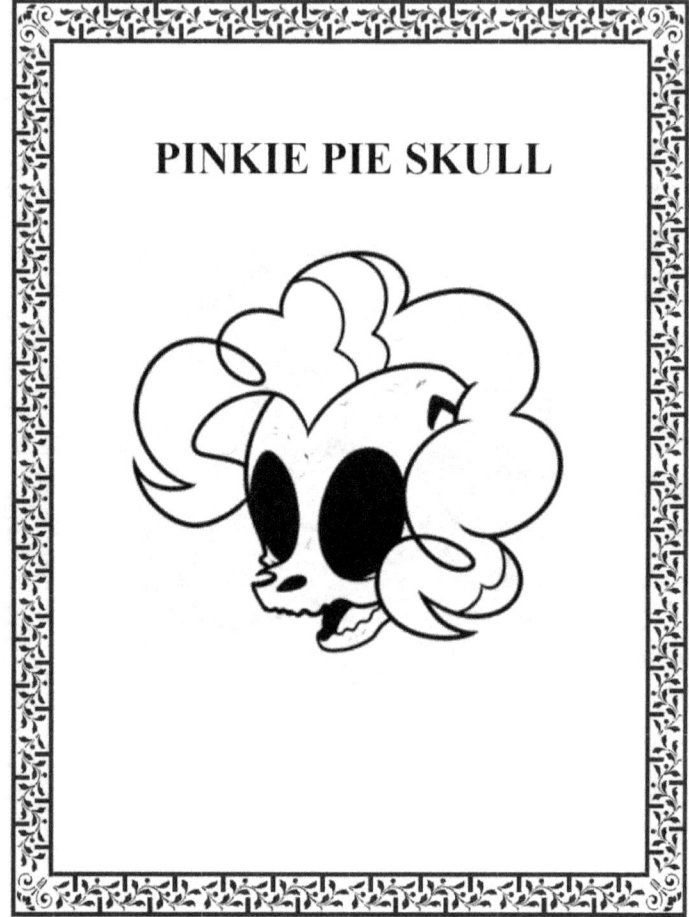

# STEP 1

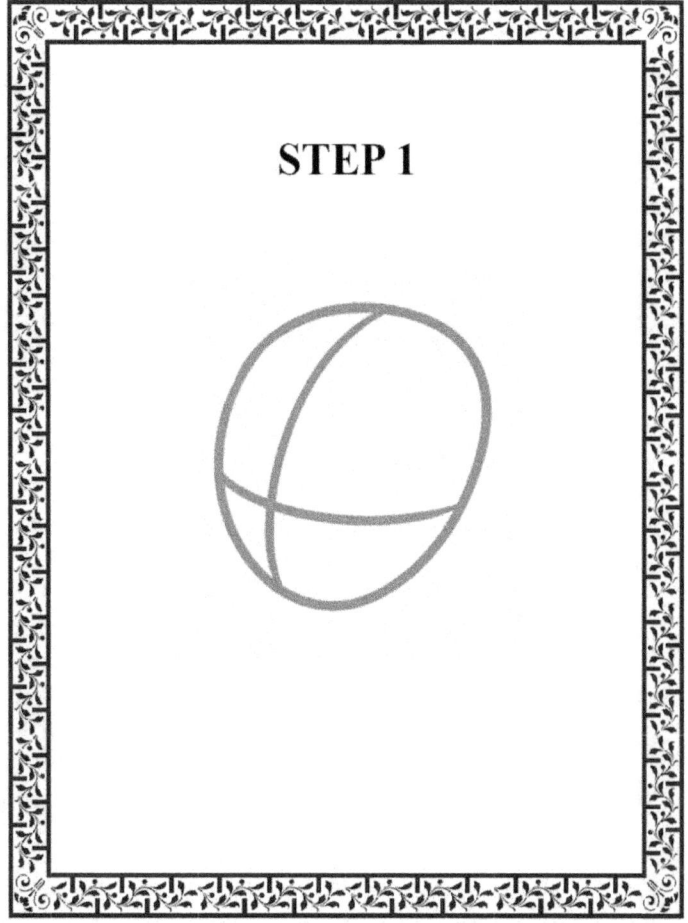

# STEP 2

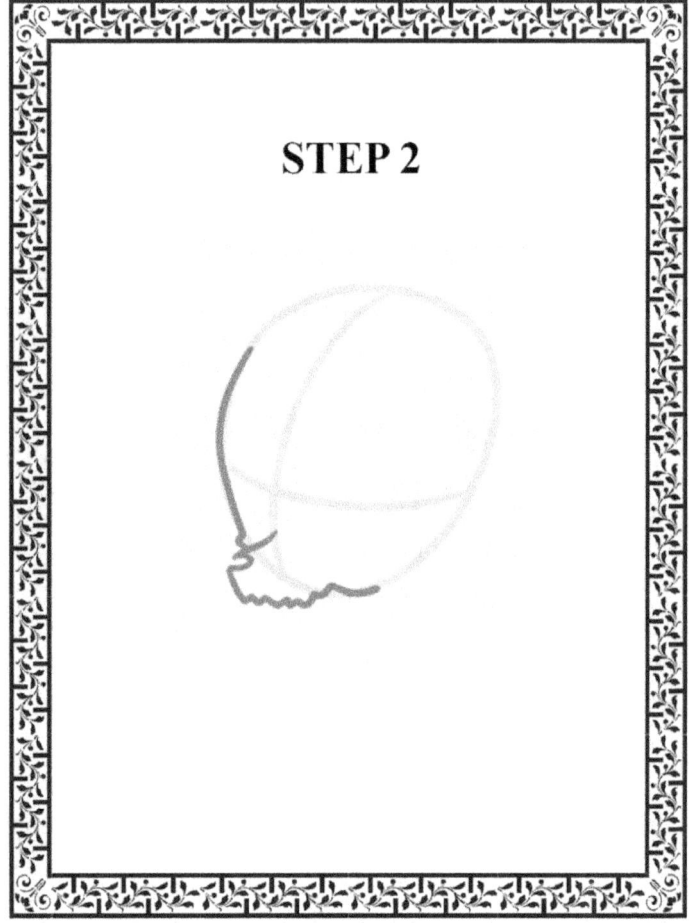

# STEP 3

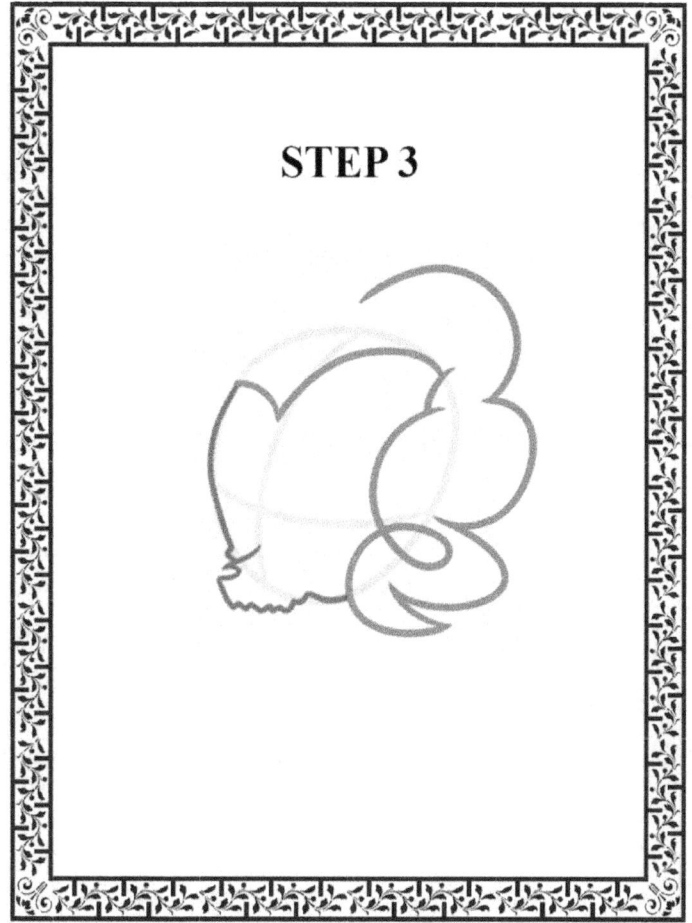

# STEP 4

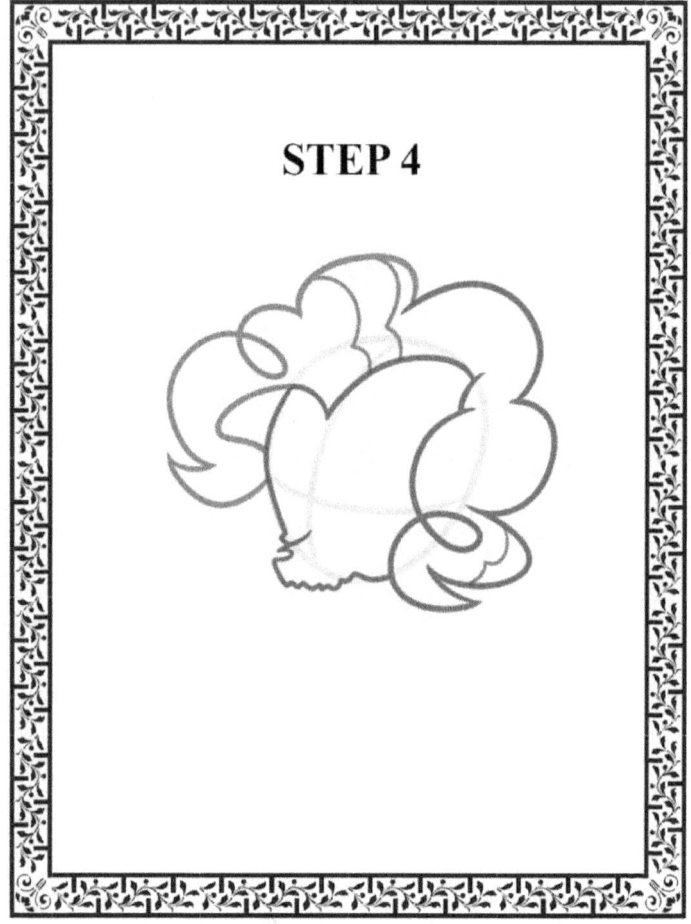

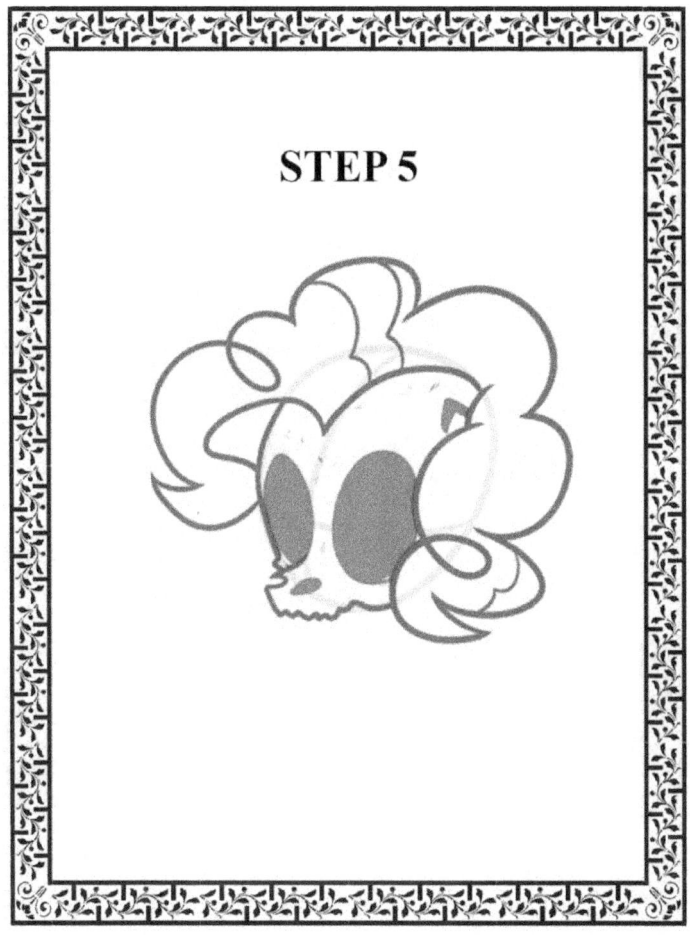

# STEP 5

# STEP 6

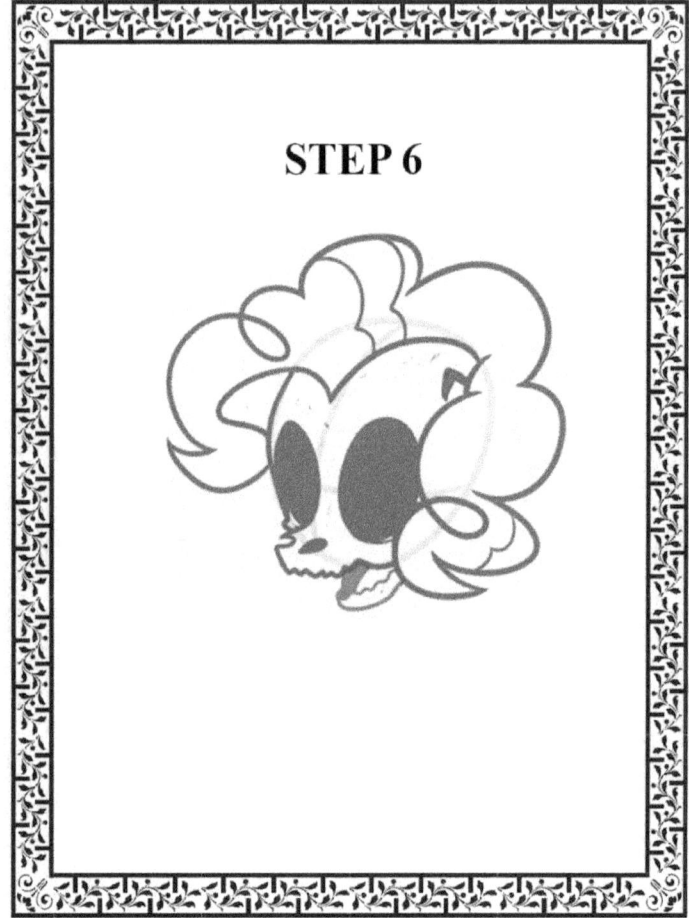

# STEP 7

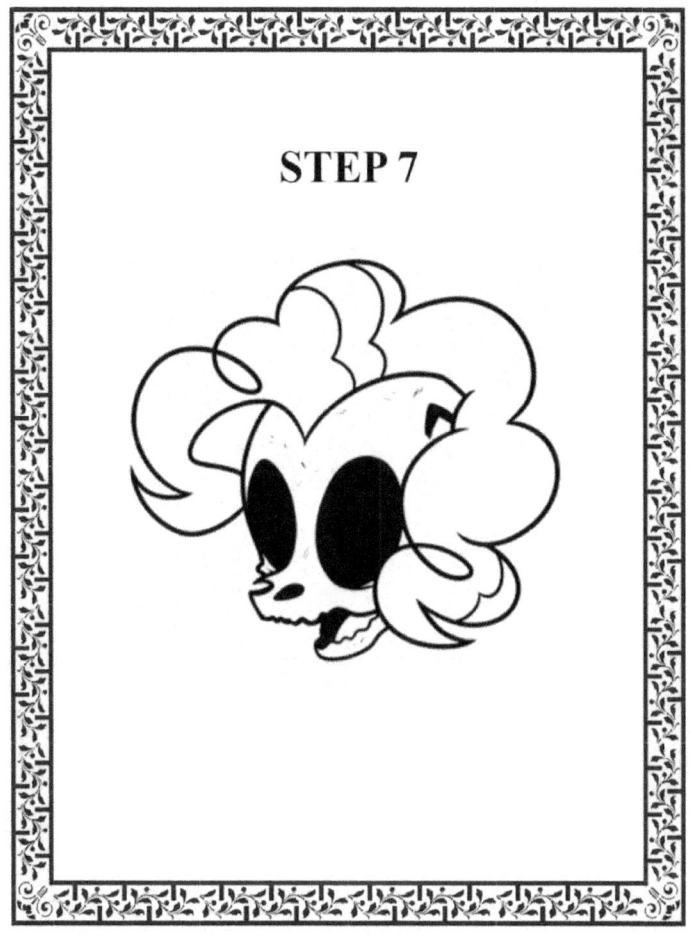

# YIN YANG SKULL

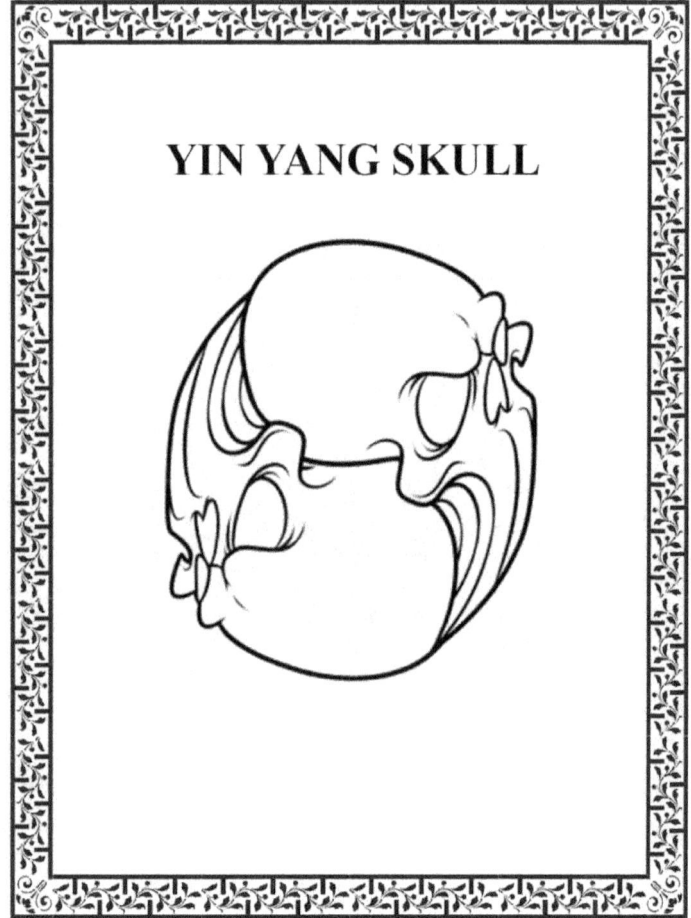

# STEP 1

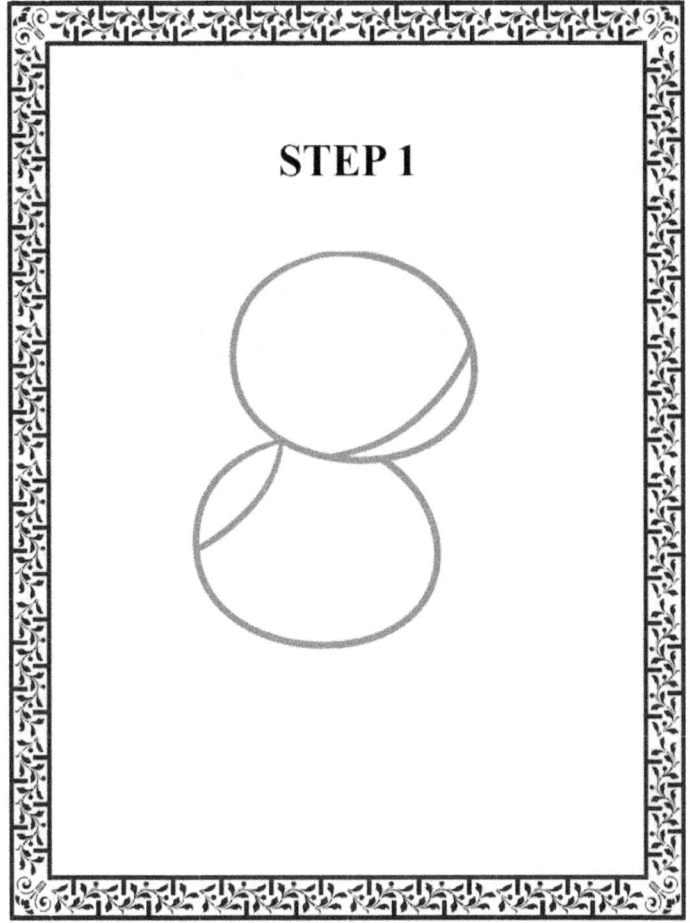

# STEP 2

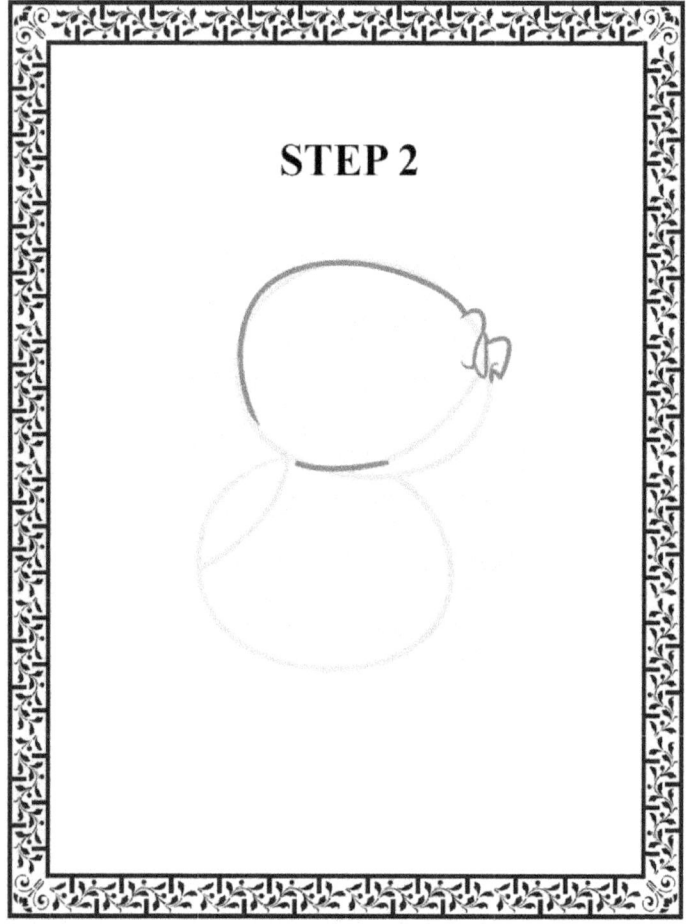

# STEP 3

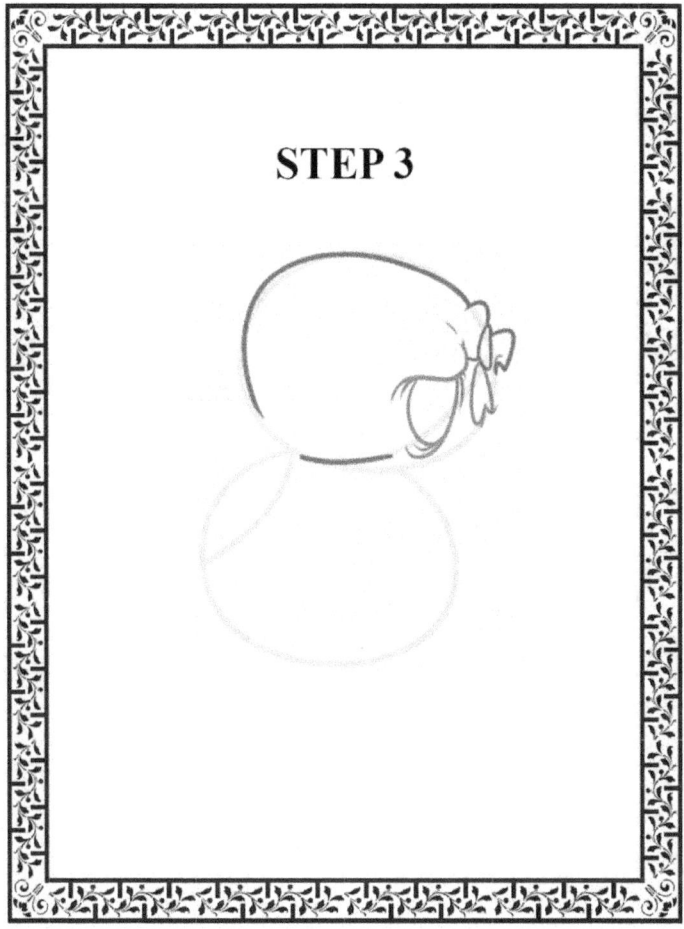

# STEP 4

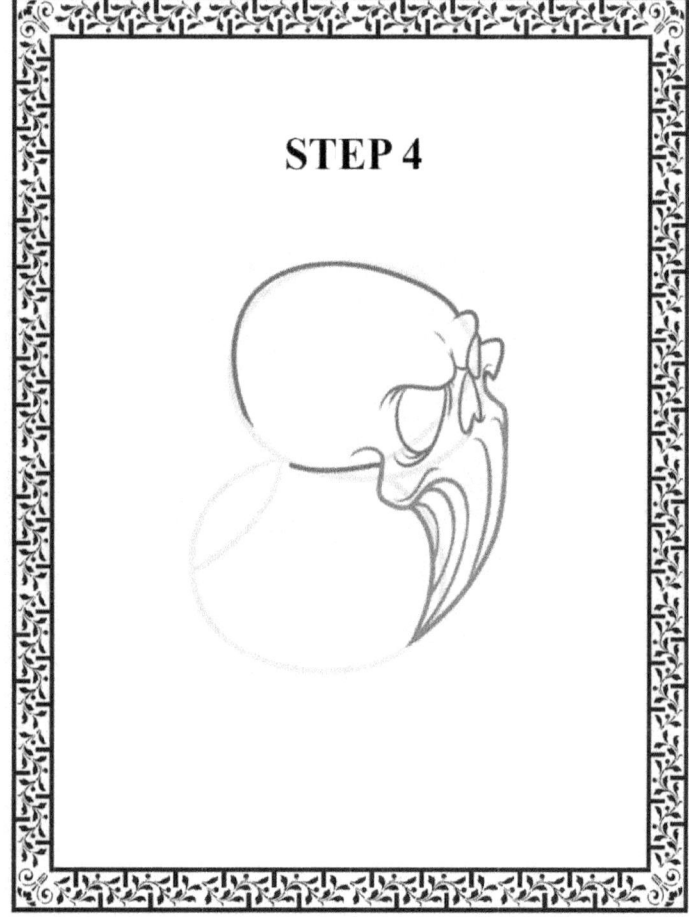

# STEP 5

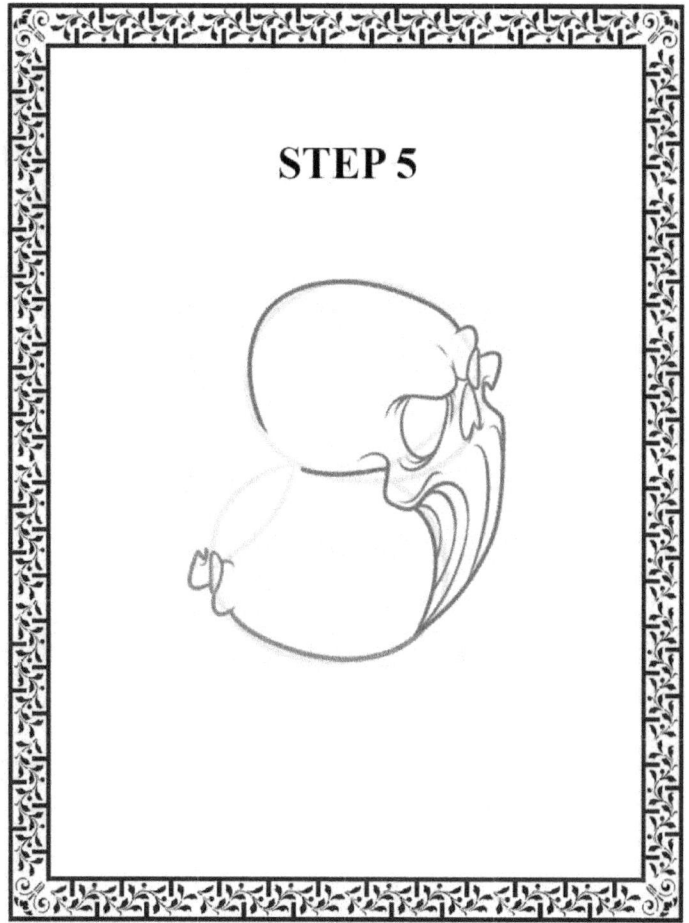

# STEP 6

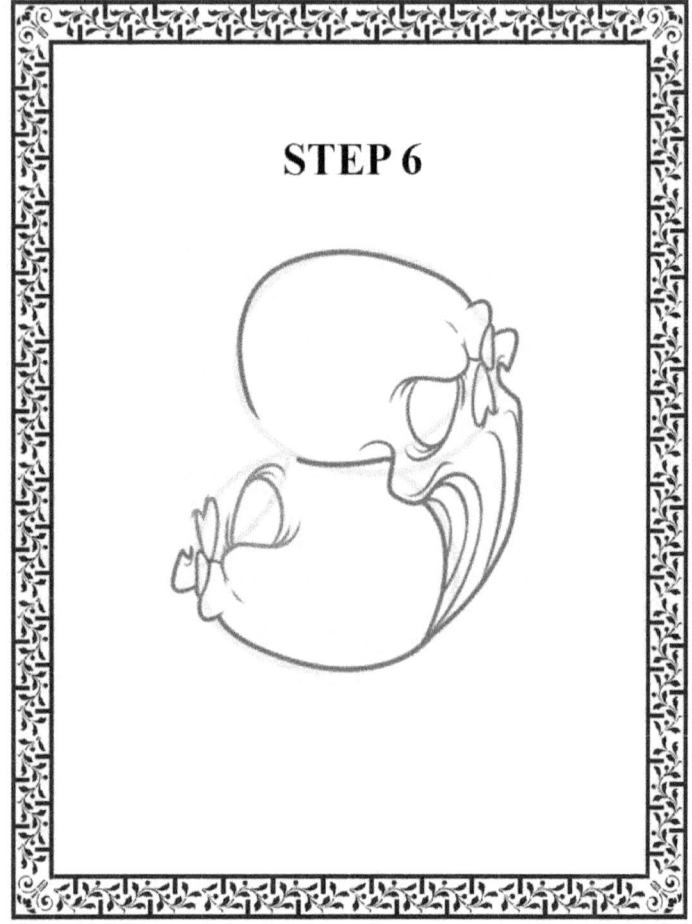

# STEP 7

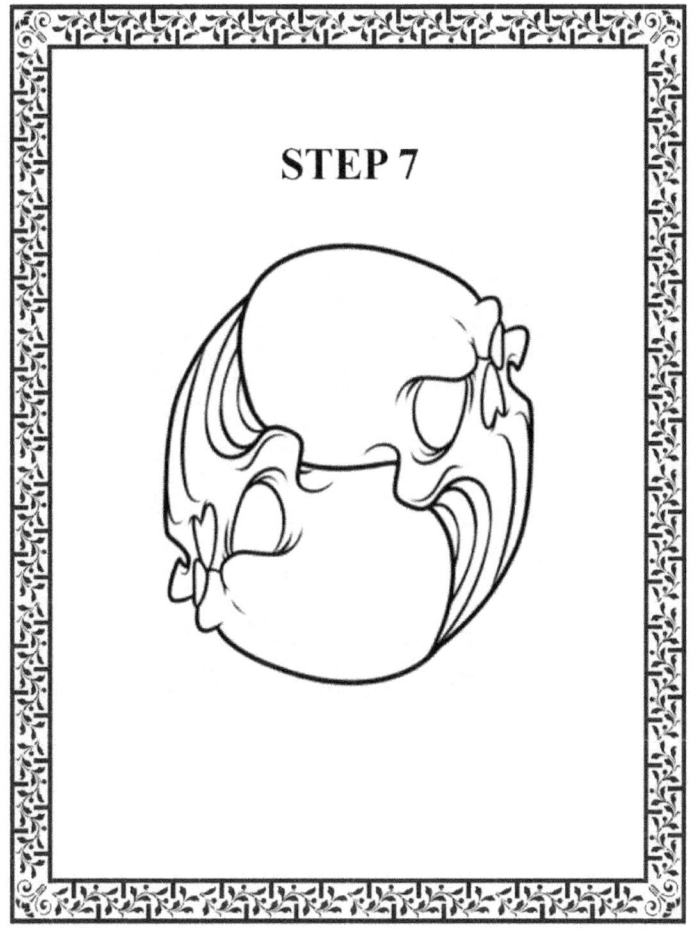